Date: 9/11/12

J 796.357 BUR
Burdick, Mason.
Baseball /

PALM BEACH COUNTY
LIBRARY SYSTEM
3650 SUMMIT BLVD.
WEST PALM BEACH, FL 33406

ON THE TEAM

BASEBALL

By Mason Burdick

Gareth Stevens
Publishing

Please visit our website, www.garethstevens.com. For a free color catalog of all our high-quality books, call toll free 1-800-542-2595 or fax 1-877-542-2596.

Library of Congress Cataloging-in-Publication Data

Burdick, Mason.
Baseball / Mason Burdick.
    p. cm. — (On the team)
Includes index.
ISBN 978-1-4339-6434-3 (pbk.)
ISBN 978-1-4339-6435-0 (6-pack)
ISBN 978-1-4339-6432-9 (library binding)
1. Baseball—Juvenile literature. I. Title.
GV867.5.B86 2012
796.357—dc23

2011018199

First Edition

Published in 2012 by
Gareth Stevens Publishing
111 East 14th Street, Suite 349
New York, NY 10003

Copyright © 2012 Gareth Stevens Publishing

Designer: Michael J. Flynn
Editor: Greg Roza

Photo credits: Cover, pp. 1, 13 Erik Isakson/Getty Images; pp. 4, 6–7, 8–9, 14–15, 18, 20, 21 Shutterstock.com; p. 5 Jim McIsaac/Getty Images; pp. 10, 17 iStockphoto.com.

All rights reserved. No part of this book may be reproduced in any form without permission in writing from the publisher, except by a reviewer.

Printed in the United States of America

CPSIA compliance information: Batch #CW12GS: For further information contact Gareth Stevens, New York, New York at 1-800-542-2595.

Contents

Play Ball! 4

America's Pastime 7

Take the Field 8

How to Play 11

Pitcher and Catcher 12

Playing the Infield 15

Playing the Outfield 16

Batters and Runners 19

The Big Leagues 20

Glossary 22

For More Information 23

Index 24

Words in the glossary appear in **bold** type the first time they are used in the text.

Play Ball!

Baseball is a bat-and-ball sport that **originated** in the United States. Today, it's popular in countries all over the world. Both kids and adults enjoy playing baseball. It can be played anywhere there's plenty of room to run and throw a ball. Some people play in an open field. Some play in a city park. Others play in a school gym.

All you really need to play baseball is a ball, a bat, a glove, and your friends!

Do you think you have what it takes to play baseball? Then get in there and play ball!

5

THE COACH'S CORNER

Baseball gear has changed greatly over the years. The glove and shoes shown here are simpler than modern baseball gear.

America's Pastime

Baseball is based on an old English game called rounders, which also used a bat and ball. Americans began playing a game similar to modern baseball in the late 1700s. The first baseball rules were recorded in 1845. At that time, players didn't even wear gloves!

Throughout the 1800s, baseball gained popularity across the United States. The rules slowly changed to those we're familiar with today. By the early 1900s, baseball had become "America's **pastime**."

Take the Field

Baseball is usually played on grass. A baseball field has a dirt path called a diamond. The four **bases** are at the corners of the diamond. At the center of the diamond is a circle of dirt where the pitcher stands. This area is called the mound because it's usually higher than the rest of the field. Two lines, called foul lines, meet at **home plate** and mark the sides of the baseball field. The outfield is the grassy area beyond the diamond.

THE COACH'S CORNER

A ball that goes outside the foul lines is a "foul ball." That means it's out of play.

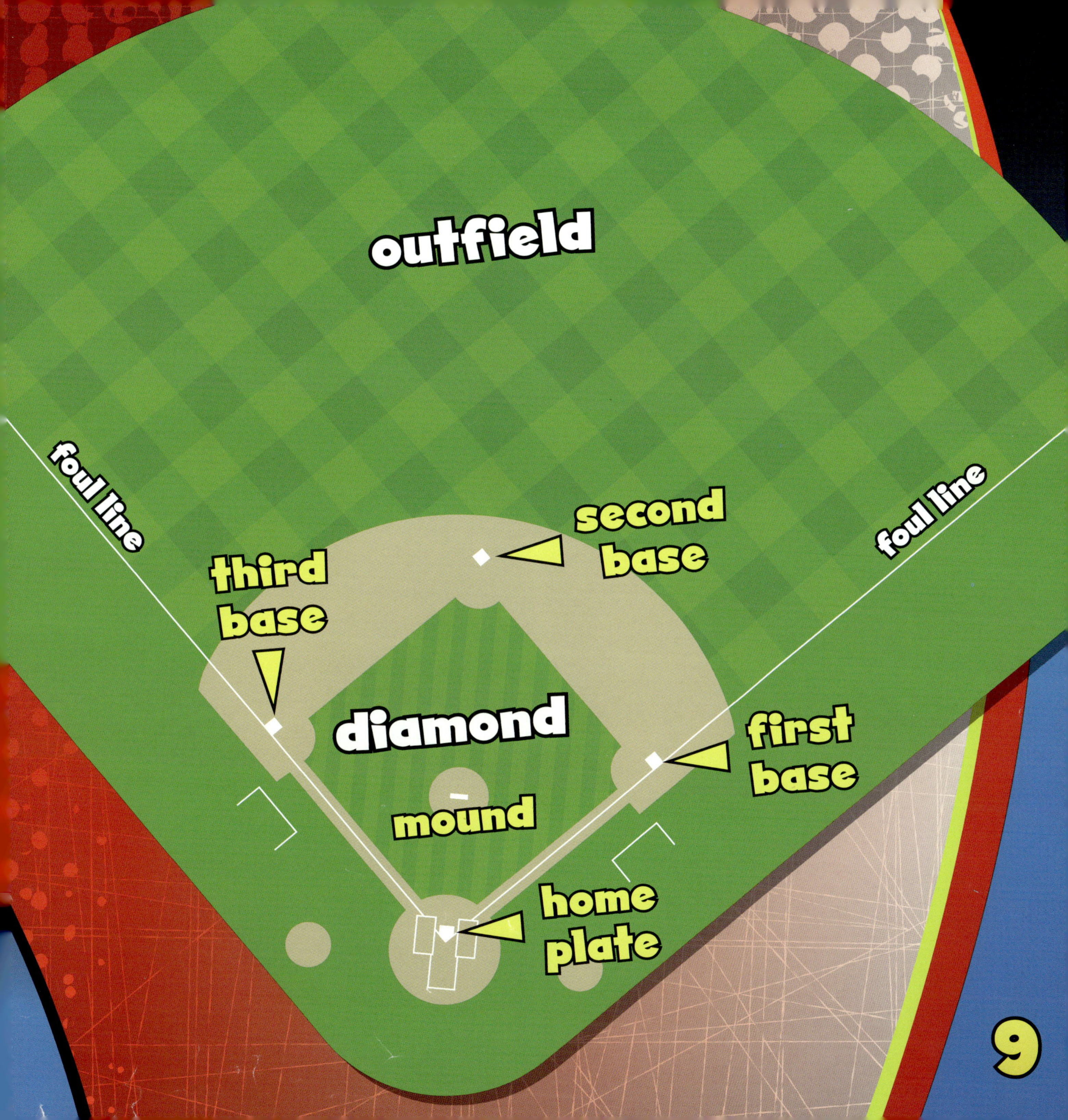

outfield

foul line

second base

third base

foul line

diamond

first base

mound

home plate

pitcher

Batters wear helmets to keep their heads safe from wild pitches.

batter

10

How to Play

A baseball game is played between two teams with nine players each. The pitcher for the team on the field tries to throw the ball past the other team's batters to his own team's catcher. That's called a "strike." A batter who gets three strikes is "out," and their turn at bat is over.

A batter who hits the ball tries to run around the bases to score points. The team on the field tries to catch the ball for an out.

THE COACH'S CORNER

When the batting team gets three outs, the teams switch sides. After both teams have had a chance at bat, the *inning* is over and the next inning begins.

Pitcher and Catcher

Every play starts when the pitcher throws the ball to the catcher. Good pitchers throw several types of pitches, such as a fastball and a curveball. Catchers use hand signs to tell pitchers what kind of pitch to throw.

The pitcher tries to throw a strike by sending the ball through the area above home plate called the strike zone. A pitch outside this area is called a ball. If a pitcher throws four balls, the batter gets to walk to first base.

THE COACH'S CORNER

When a batter hits the ball, the pitcher and catcher must help their teammates try to stop the other team from scoring points.

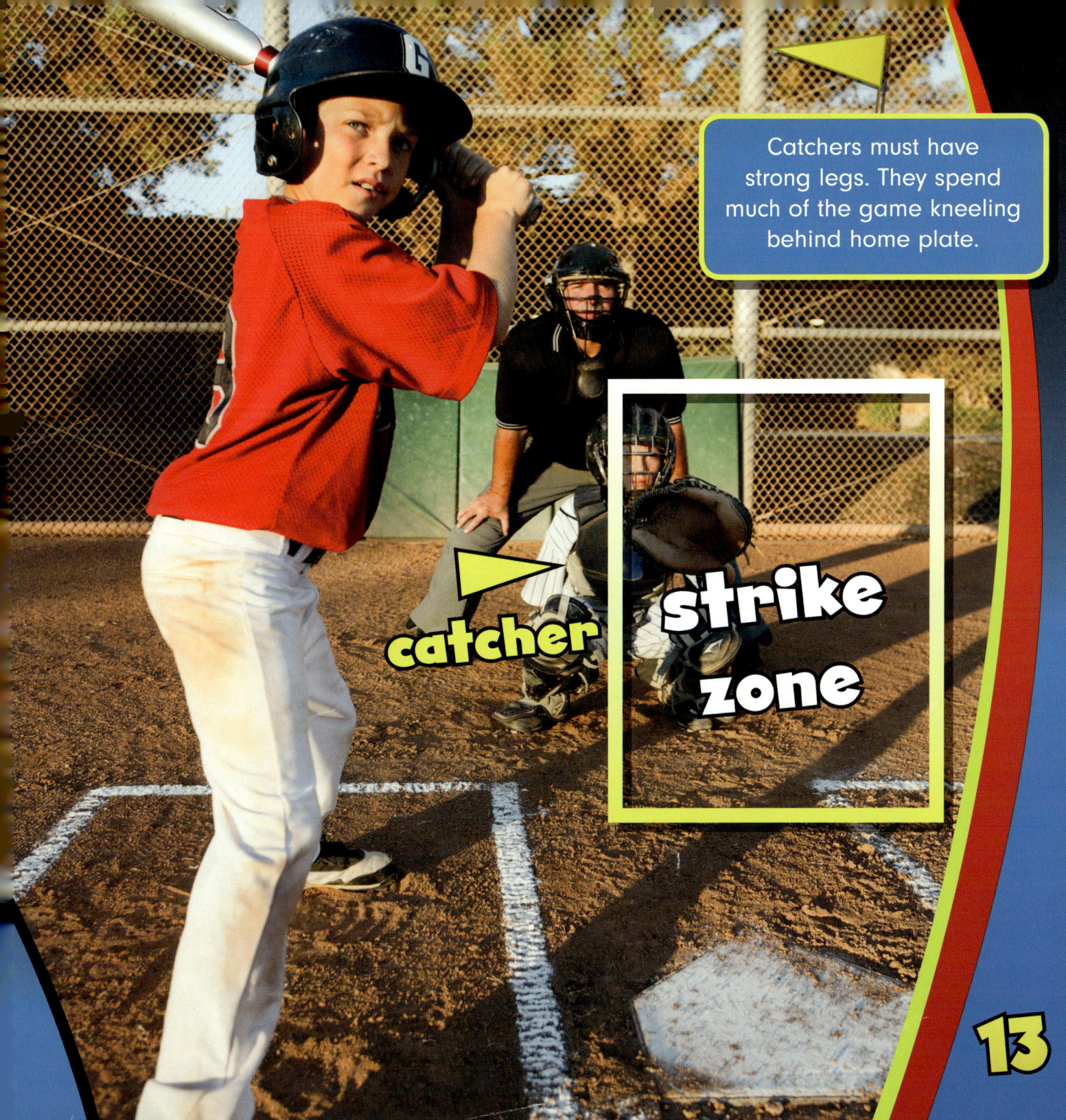

Catchers must have strong legs. They spend much of the game kneeling behind home plate.

catcher

strike zone

13

Playing the Infield

The infield is the area in and around the diamond. Besides the pitcher and catcher, there are four other players in the infield. The first baseman, second baseman, and third baseman guard the bases they're named after. The shortstop plays between second base and third base.

Infielders stop balls from going into the outfield. They make outs by catching a ball that's been hit and throwing it to a baseman before the runner reaches the base. They can get a runner out by touching them with the ball, too.

THE COACH'S CORNER

Infielders must be good at catching and throwing the ball quickly. The more *accurate* they are, the more outs they get.

Playing the Outfield

Outfielders include the right fielder, center fielder, and left fielder. They guard the large open area beyond the infield. That's a lot of space for three players to guard! They must run long distances to get the ball. They also have to make long, powerful throws to infielders to help stop runners from scoring.

Outfielders can make an out by catching a ball that hasn't bounced yet. They also chase balls that get past the infield players.

THE COACH'S CORNER

Outfielders often call out "I got it!" before catching a ball. They do that so two players don't run into each other while trying to catch the same ball!

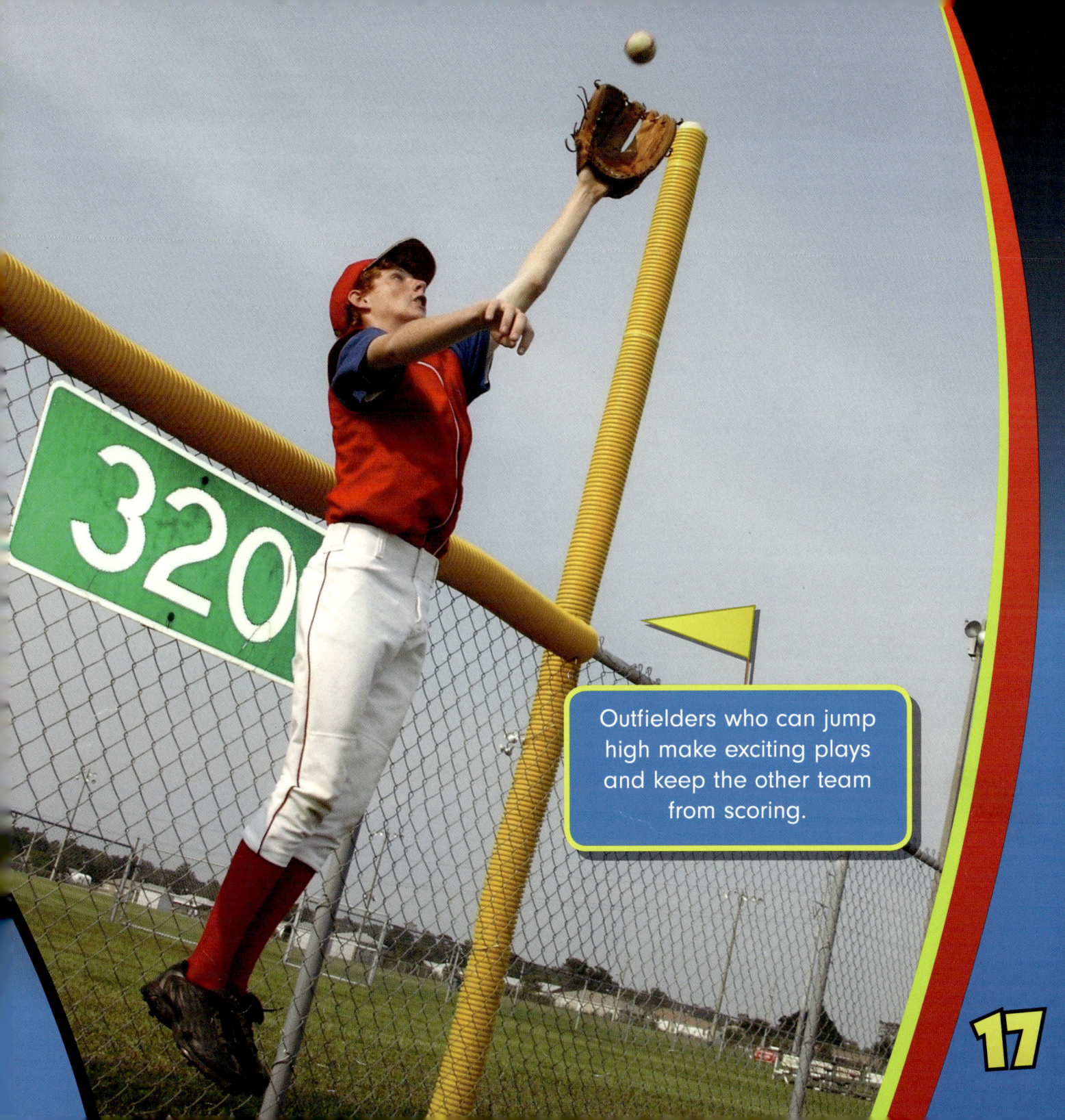

Outfielders who can jump high make exciting plays and keep the other team from scoring.

The way a batter stands while waiting for the pitch is called a stance.

18

Batters and Runners

The batter stands at home plate just in front of the other team's catcher. The batter tries to hit the ball to an area where the players on the field won't be able to catch it.

After hitting the ball, the batter becomes a runner. To score a point, a runner must touch each base and make it back to home plate without being put out by the other team. Some runners are so fast they can **steal** bases!

THE COACH'S CORNER

Sometimes a batter makes it around all the bases in one play. That's a home run. When a batter hits a home run, any runner already on base makes it to home plate, too!

The Big Leagues

Baseball is a game that just about anyone can play for fun. However, some people make a living playing it.

In the United States and Canada, Major League Baseball (MLB) is the highest level of **professional** baseball. There are 30 teams in the MLB. Each team has players who've been playing baseball their whole lives. If you work hard and practice, you might play professional baseball one day, too!

Baseball Gear

bat	• most are wood • some are made of a light metal called aluminum • between 24 and 34 inches (61 and 86 cm) long
ball	• cork center wrapped in yarn • covered with two pieces of leather that are sewn together • weighs between 5 and 5.25 ounces (141.7 and 148.8 g) • between 9 and 9.25 inches (22.86 and 23.5 cm) around
glove	• made mostly of leather • an oil is used to make the leather soft so it bends more easily
batting helmet	• made of hard plastic
catcher's mask	• metal cage worn over face

Glossary

accurate: free from mistakes

base: one of the four stations a runner must touch at the corners of a baseball diamond

home plate: the base where a batter stands while batting and the last base a runner touches to score a run

inning: a part of a baseball game during which each team bats until it gets three outs

originate: start

pastime: an activity that someone enjoys during their free time

professional: earning money from an activity that many people do for fun

steal: to run from one base to another before the pitcher throws the ball

For More Information

Books

Buckley, James E. *Baseball.* New York, NY: DK Publishing, 2010.

Jacobs, Greg. *The Everything Kids' Baseball Book: From Baseball History to Player Stats—With Lots of Homerun Fun in Between!* Avon, MA: Adams Media, 2010.

Websites

Baseball Rules & Regulations
www.baseball-almanac.com/rulemenu.shtml
Read more about the rules of baseball, including how they have changed over time.

Safety Tips: Baseball
kidshealth.org/parent/firstaid_safe/outdoor/safety_baseball.html
Learn how to be safe while playing baseball.

Publisher's note to educators and parents: Our editors have carefully reviewed these websites to ensure that they are suitable for students. Many websites change frequently, however, and we cannot guarantee that a site's future contents will continue to meet our high standards of quality and educational value. Be advised that students should be closely supervised whenever they access the Internet.

Index

ball 4, 7, 11, 12, 15, 16, 19, 21
baseman 14, 15
bases 8, 9, 11, 12, 15, 19
bat 4, 7, 11, 21
batter 10, 11, 12, 18, 19
catcher 11, 12, 13, 14, 15, 19
catcher's mask 21
diamond 8, 9, 15
foul ball 8
foul lines 8, 9
gear 6, 21
glove 4, 6, 7, 21
helmet 10, 21
home plate 8, 9, 12, 13, 19
home run 19
infield 15, 16
infielders 15, 16
inning 11
Major League Baseball (MLB) 20
mound 8, 9
out 11, 15, 16, 19
outfield 8, 9, 15, 16
outfielders 16, 17
pitcher 8, 10, 11, 12, 14, 15
pitches 10, 12, 18
rounders 7
runner 15, 16, 19
shortstop 14, 15
steal 19
strike 11, 12
strike zone 12, 13